Sugar

The story of sugar goes back to prehistoric times when men and women gathered fruits for their sweet taste. But for thousands of years honey was the only known sweetener. Sugar from cane was not grown until about 5,000 years ago. For many centuries sugar was a rare luxury which only the very rich could afford. But gradually it spread to many different lands until today it is a multi-million pound industry and sugar is within the reach of all to enjoy. This easy access to the delights of sugar has brought with it many health problems. In clear and simple language and with the aid of many coloured illustrations, the author traces the life-cycle of sugar cane and sugar beet – the two main sources of sugar. He describes how the farmer nurtures his crop until it is ready for harvesting and then the various processes it must pass through to extract the sugar. He shows how sugar is not only used in the food and drink industry but is also used in medicine and in the chemical industry. Alan Blackwood was an editor of children's books before becoming a freelance author. He has written numerous books for a variety of publishers.

Focus on
SUGAR

Alan Blackwood

Focus on Resources series

Alternative Energy
Coffee
Cotton
Dairy Produce
Gas
Grain
Nuclear Fuel
Oil
Seafood
Sugar
Tea
Timber
Water
Wool

Frontispiece *Sugar cane plantations on the island of Fiji, in the Pacific Ocean.*

First published in 1985 by
Wayland (Publishers) Ltd
61 Western Road, Hove
East Sussex BN3 1JD, England

© Copyright 1985 Wayland (Publishers) Ltd

Phototypeset by Kalligraphics Ltd, Redhill, Surrey
Printed in Italy by G. Canale & C.S.p.A., Turin
Bound in Great Britain at The Bath Press, Avon

British Library Cataloguing in Publication Data

Blackwood, Alan
 Focus on sugar. – (Focus on resources)
 1. Sugar – Juvenile literature
 I. Title   II. Series
 641.3'36   TX560.S9

 ISBN 0–85078–618–5

Contents

1. What is sugar?

Sugar is high in calories and easily and quickly digested, so it gives us almost instant energy for playing sports like football.

The dictionary describes sugar as 'a crystalline substance with a sweet taste'. It is, of course, this sweet taste that appeals to us.

Sugar not only tastes good, it is also, in moderation, an important foodstuff. It belongs to a large group of foods called carbohydrates. Another name for them is sugars and starches. Bread, cereals, including rice and potatoes, are all carbohydrate foods.

Their chief food value is in providing us with energy. This energy value is measured as calories, or the amount of heat produced in the body that can be used as energy. Sugar is very high in calories. Moreover, it is very easily and quickly digested so it gives us almost instant energy — for thinking hard as well as walking or

Above *A small selection of the many foods and drinks which contain carbohydrates.*

running. This is why chocolate, which is full of sugar, is included in survival kits and emergency rations. It takes up hardly any space, while packing a lot of food energy.

Too much sugar, though, is not good for you. Refined sugar is bad for the teeth. It combines with bacteria in the mouth to form an acid that attacks the protective enamel on our teeth and leads to their decay. Cleaning the teeth, especially after eating sweet things, can help prevent this. And, as we shall read in Chapter 14, eating too much sugary food can be bad in other ways too. Many people in Britain and other Western countries are overweight because they eat too much sugar, which can lead to serious health problems.

Below *Eating too many carbohydrates in your diet can lead to being overweight.*

7

2. Where does sugar come from?

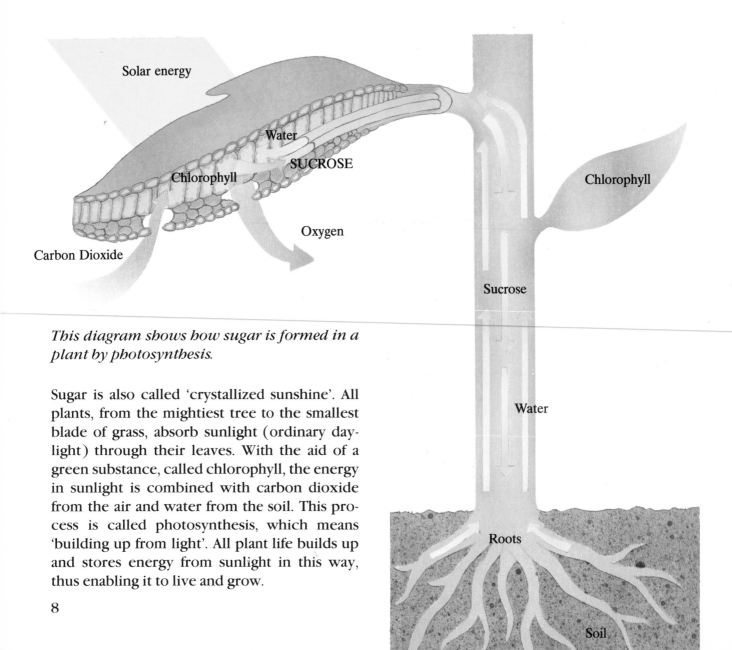

This diagram shows how sugar is formed in a plant by photosynthesis.

Sugar is also called 'crystallized sunshine'. All plants, from the mightiest tree to the smallest blade of grass, absorb sunlight (ordinary daylight) through their leaves. With the aid of a green substance, called chlorophyll, the energy in sunlight is combined with carbon dioxide from the air and water from the soil. This process is called photosynthesis, which means 'building up from light'. All plant life builds up and stores energy from sunlight in this way, thus enabling it to live and grow.

8

Sugar gives the sweet taste to these fruits on sale at a roadside stall in the Caribbean.

This energy is stored in the form of starches and many varieties of sugar. Scientists class these sugars under such headings as sucrose, glucose or dextrose, fructose and lactose. By eating plants as vegetables, we digest a part of their own store of solar energy, although we do not tend to think of such plants as sugary.

We are much more aware of the sugar in plants when we eat sweet, juicy fruits such as apples, pears, plums, peaches and grapes; or eat the honey that bees have made from the sweetish nectar of flowers. The sap of the maple tree, and of some types of corn, including one called sorghum, also provide sweet natural syrups.

But our main source of sugar is from sugar cane and sugar beet. It is these two plants that between them give us the sugar – the 'crystallized sunshine' – we all know and enjoy.

Below *Sugar cane or* saccharum officinarum, *to give it its proper scientific name.*

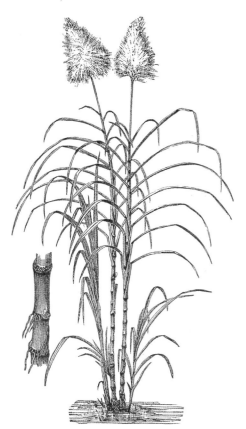

3. Growing sugar cane

The scientific Latin name for sugar cane is *saccharum officinarum*. It is a giant variety of grass, like bamboo. It has a tall, thick, jointed stem, with a top or crown of long, grassy leaves, and grows to a height of 4 to 6 metres (13 to 20 feet). It is the sap (the fluid) in the long stem — the cane — that contains the high concentration of natural sugars.

Sugar cane grows in warm or hot regions of the world, where there is also adequate rainfall. At one time, the islands of the Caribbean produced most of the cane used in the sugar industry. Today, it is widely cultivated in Central and South America, Africa, Pakistan, India and Sri

This map shows the areas of the world where sugar cane and sugar beet are cultivated.

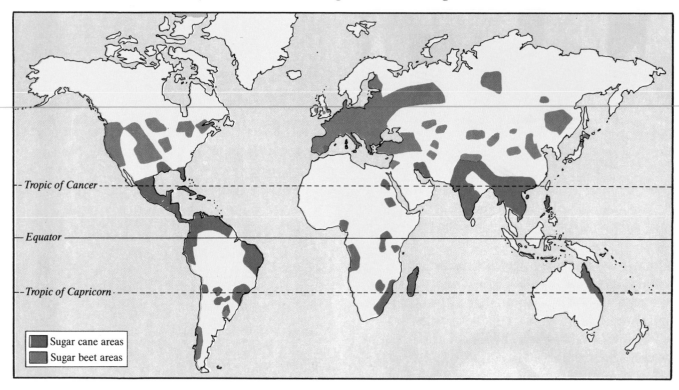

Tropic of Cancer

Equator

Tropic of Capricorn

Sugar cane areas
Sugar beet areas

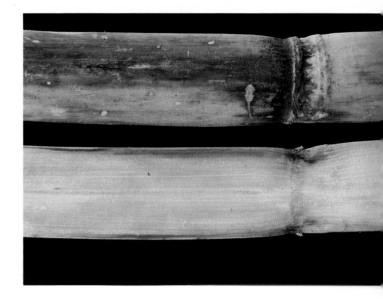

Lanka, the Far East and Australia.

Sugar cane may be grown from seeds produced by the large 'flower', or tassel, that sprouts from the top of each plant if it is left alone. Usually, though, seeds are only used in nurseries to develop new varieties of the plant. On plantations and farms a much easier method is used. Cuttings taken from existing cane are laid in shallow furrows in the ground and covered with a thin layer of soil. All being well, these cuttings, or 'setts', will soon take root along the joints, or the 'nodes', of the cane, and green shoots will sprout from the soil. A new crop is then on its way.

Below *Cuttings of sugar cane being prepared for planting on the island of Mauritius.*

4. From seed to healthy plant

Sugar cane flowering on a plantation in the state of Queensland in Australia.

Above *Fields of young sugar cane.*

Sugar cane grows quickly, reaching its full height in about a year. As it grows, the long blades of leaf wither and drop off the cane, and new ones sprout from the top.

The planter or farmer, though, cannot just stand idly by. Depending on the climate, he may need to irrigate his plantation, to ensure that the cane receives enough water throughout its growing period, otherwise it will not yield enough sugar. Ideally, growing cane should receive some water every day. On the other hand, too much heavy tropical rain can saturate the earth, and make the cane rot in the ground.

In this case, the planter may need to organize and maintain drainage schemes.

Farmers must also guard against certain plant diseases and pests. White leaf, red stripe, yellow spot — all named after the effect they have on the cane — are three diseases that can ruin a crop. Locusts (a particular menace in parts of Africa), rats and caterpillars can also cause great damage by eating the leaves or burrowing into the cane itself. Chemical sprays can protect cane against a good deal of such damage. And new varieties of cane are being developed that are resistant to such forms of attack.

Below *An irrigation scheme in the Sudan for watering fields of sugar cane.*

5. Gathering the crop

Harvesting sugar cane in the traditional way, using a special long knife, called a machete.

There is no special season for harvesting sugar cane. Some farmers gather it in after it has been growing for about a year and has reached a height of 4 or 5 metres (13 to 16 feet). By then, the actual cane is roughly 3 centimetres (just over 1 inch) across and is hard and yellow in appearance. Its sugar content is about 15 per cent of the plant's total weight. Other farmers wait longer, hoping for the cane to grow a bit more and accumulate even more sugar. Sometimes the plants eventually fall over, due to their own height and weight.

The traditional way to harvest cane was to cut it down close to the ground, then trim off the leaves, using a special long knife called a machete. Some farmers working smallholdings still go about their work in this way. On most plantations today, however, the cane is cut, trimmed and delivered straight into waiting trucks by big mechanical harvesters.

Another old practice is to set fire to the cane fields just before harvesting. The fire burns off the leaves without damaging the hard, thick cane. This saves the farmer a good deal of hard work, and at the same time it cleanses the fields of many pests and diseases. But burning the cane also produces thick clouds of smoke, and in some countries anti-pollution laws now forbid this being done.

Above   *Harvesting sugar cane the modern way on a plantation in Queensland, Australia.*
Below   *Just before harvesting, the cane is sometimes set on fire to remove the unwanted leaves.*

6. Sugar beet – the adaptable root

This cross-section of a field of sugar beet shows that it is a root vegetable. The large roots store the sugar.

16

A field of sugar cane in East Anglia, England.

Sugar beet on sale in Beijing (Peking), China.

Sugar beet (*beta vulgaris* or *beta maritima*) is a very different kind of plant from sugar cane. It is a root vegetable, like the turnip, parsnip, carrot and beetroot.

It has a natural two-year growing cycle. In the first year it builds up its store of sugar, and in the second, if it is left in the ground, it produces seeds. It is the large root – weighing on average 1 kilogram (about 2 lb) – that stores the sugar. As a part of this process, the plant absorbs around 60 litres (13 gallons) of water during the main growing season.

Large fields of sugar beet, looking rather like cabbages, are a common sight in parts of Britain, especially East Anglia. This indicates that it is a crop belonging to the temperate regions of the world – places with fairly warm summers and cool or cold winters. All the same, it has proved very adaptable to different climates. In Europe, for example, it can grow almost equally well as far south as Sicily and as far north as Finland. It is also grown in large areas of the USSR and China, the USA and Canada, and in parts of Argentina and Chile.

17

7. Growing sugar beet

Most farmers grow sugar beet in rotation with other crops, such as wheat and barley. They switch their crops from field to field, year by year, so that no one crop exhausts the soil of particular minerals or other nutrients.

The beet is planted in the spring. Unlike cane, it is grown from seed. In the past, seeds often produced two or three young plants each, and the farmer had the back-breaking job of thinning them out. Modern varieties of seed, however, produce only one plant, and machines now 'drill' each seed into the soil in evenly spaced rows.

Farmers still have to contend with the weather, however. If the spring is too cold or too dry, the seeds may not germinate. If it rains

Preparing the soil before sowing the seeds of sugar beet.

too hard, they may start to grow and then rot.

Through the summer months, while the crop is growing, there are plenty of other jobs for the farmer. Fields need regular weeding using mechanical hoes that break up the soil between the rows of beet, or by spraying weedkiller.

There are also pests and diseases to watch out for. 'Virus yellow' is spread by flies that suck sap from the leaves, turn them yellow and stop them making the sugar for the root to store. A type of caterpillar, called a cutworm, burrows into the soil and eats away at the roots. Chemicals can protect the beet from these pests, though the farmer must beware in case they damage his crops as well.

Below *Spraying a chemical weedkiller between the rows of young sugar beet plants.*

8. From field to factory

Harvest-time for sugar beet is late summer, or early autumn, just before the beet starts living off its own store of sugar. Once again, the farmer keeps an anxious eye on the weather. Heavy rain can turn the beet fields into mud, making it difficult or impossible for machines to operate. In northern countries where beet is grown —

This harvesting machine cuts off the top of the beet at the same time as lifting the root.

Harvested sugar beet on a farm in Italy.

Scotland, Finland, Sweden, and parts of the USSR – there is also the risk that winter may arrive early and freeze the beet into the ground.

Today harvesting is mostly done mechanically in two stages. One machine first moves down the rows of beet, slicing off the 'crown' of each plant – the very top of the root just below the leaves. A second machine then lifts the rest of the root out of the ground. Mechanical sieves shake off the heaviest clods of earth, and the freshly harvested crop is loaded on to farm wagons.

Some of the beet may be delivered straight to the factory, to be processed into sugar. But the farmer does not have to dispose of his crop all at once. He can store it in 'clamps' – big piles of beet covered with bales of straw or plastic sheeting to protect them from the weather – until it is convenient for him to make further deliveries to the factory.

9. Extracting the sugar

Sugar can be eaten straight from sugar cane. But the sugar we are familiar with has gone through a long process of extraction and refinement before we get hold of it.

When it arrives at the processing factory, the sugar cane is treated in one of two ways. It may be cut up into sections and fed through powerful rolling mills that squeeze out the sap, or juice, which is then dissolved in water.

Alternatively, it may be fed into a machine that first chops it up and shreds it into little pieces. The shreds of cane then pass into special tanks, called 'diffusers', where strong jets of hot water wash out the juice. The resulting solution of sugar juice in water may be pumped through the 'diffusers' several times, extracting a little more juice from the cane each time, and so adding to the strength of the solution. (At the end of the whole process, factories take care that the water they return to rivers and lakes is sugar-free, since sugar reduces the oxygen content in water, which can lead to the death of fish and plant life.)

Meanwhile, little or nothing is wasted in the sugar industry. The residue of squeezed-out and washed-out cane is called by the French word *bagasse*. Some factories use it as fuel to heat more water and help drive the machinery. It also has many other valuable applications as we shall read on page 35.

Cane being chopped up and shredded inside a processing factory on the island of Barbados.

Harvested sugar cane arriving at a processing factory on the island of Fiji.

10. Making the sugar

The first solution of cane sugar juice from the rollers or 'diffusers' is dark and cloudy with impurities. To get rid of these, it is poured into other tanks, called 'clarifiers', where lime is added. The lime combines chemically with many of the impurities to form a thick sludge on the bottom of the tanks.

When this sludge has been drained off, the purer sugar solution is fed into 'evaporators' — special boilers that boil down or reduce the

Mini-mountains of raw sugar in a warehouse, waiting for refining into white sugar.

Above *A row of centrifugal machines which separate the crystals of the* massecuite.

Below *The 'evaporator' on the left reduces the water content in the sugar solution.*

water content, until the solution becomes a concentrated sugary syrup.

The next step is to turn the sugar in the syrup into crystals. This is done by 'seeding' the syrup with existing sugar crystals. These encourage the high sugar concentration to 'precipitate' – to form new crystals. The resulting mixture of thick dark syrup and sugar crystals is called *massecuite*, another French word, which means 'cooked mass'.

Separating the newly formed crystals from the syrup is done by a machine called a centrifugal. It spins the *massecuite* round in a drum, throwing it outwards by centrifugal force against the sides of the drum, much as a spindrier treats newly washed clothes. The sugar crystals collect on the sides of the drum, while the very dark and sweet syrup, now called molasses, is drained away.

25

11. Further processing

The raw sugar crystals taken from the centrifugal are still coated with a film of molasses. At this stage they give us a traditional type of brown sugar called demerara – named after a town in Guyana, South America.

This is the form in which most sugar is shipped in bulk from the producing countries to customers overseas. Much of it is then further refined. The raw sugar is first soaked in another thick syrup. This already contains such a high

A cargo of raw sugar from the Caribbean being unloaded.

concentration of sugar that it cannot dissolve any more crystals. But it does remove the coating of molasses. Centrifugals then separate the cleaned-up crystals from the syrup. The process is called affination.

The crystals are dissolved once more, for final purification, then returned to their crystalline state. So we end up with the refined white sugar – almost pure sucrose – familiar to us all.

In the centre of the picture is a sugar refinery on the River Thames in London.

Brown sugars, including today most so-called 'demerara' sugar, are made by returning to the crystals some of the molasses and syrups already removed. The molasses and syrups themselves can also be further refined, to give us various brands of treacle.

12. Refining sugar beet

Processed beet for animal fodder being ejected from a factory in northern France.

Unlike the natural juice of cane sugar, raw sugar beet is not good to eat. But the end product made from it – refined white sugar – is almost exactly the same.

On arrival at the factory, each delivery of beet is weighed, and the farmer paid accordingly.

Today, samples are also analysed for sugar content, and how much the farmer is paid may also depend on the sugar yield of his crop.

A good way to shift the great piles of heavy, bulky beet is with powerful jets of water. These send them tumbling into troughs or channels of water, called 'flumes', by which they are conveyed, floating and bobbing along into the factory. All this water also cleans them of remaining earth and stones.

The beet is sliced up by machines into strips, or cossettes. These are softened by hot water, then fed into diffusers, where more streams of water extract the sugar and dissolve it, in exactly the same way as that applied to cane. In fact, some diffusers are now designed to deal with either cane or beet.

The used-up cossettes are removed from the diffusers and often squeezed into a pulp to form the basis of cattle feed. Meanwhile, the strong sugar solution is treated with lime and other chemicals to remove impurities, then boiled up, reduced and converted into crystals, in the same way as sugar cane is treated.

A sugar beet factory in Norfolk, England.

13. Sugar in food and drinks

We buy sugar in a wide variety of forms. Among the white refined sugars there is granulated, the all-purpose grade; sugar lumps or cubes, specially made for coffee and tea; caster sugar, with smaller crystals or grains than granulated; icing sugar, made by crushing the crystals to a powder; and preserving sugar, with extra large crystals, which dissolve slowly and act with the pectin in fruit, so helping jam to set. In addition, there are the brown sugars and treacles and such fancy products as the large gem-like lumps of sugar called coffee crystals.

Today there is a vast range of foodstuffs and

Most of our food and drinks contain sugar.

Sugar is used in baking bread.

drinks containing sugar. We can easily draw up a list of some of these: chocolates, toffees and sweets, many soft drinks, ice cream, custard, cakes, buns and biscuits, jellies and blancmanges, caramels and meringues.

The list of foods containing sugar does not end there. Today, an estimated 70 per cent of all foodstuffs are processed in some way, giving us almost the same wide choice of foods and drinks throughout the year. Sugar plays a part in the processing and the preserving of canned or frozen vegetables, soups, sausages and cooked meats, and some cheeses. It is present, too, in most ketchups, sauces and mayonnaises.

Bakers use sugar as well. It acts with yeast to leaven, or activate, the dough and make the bread rise in the oven. Most cake mixes include sugar, which traps air in the mix during baking, so giving a light and fluffy texture to the cake.

31

14. Sugar and your body

We have already noted how sugar sweetens many soft drinks. In the manufacture of wines, beers and spirits it acts with an enzyme (a chemical agent) in yeast to form alcohol. This chemical action is called fermentation.

In the case of wine made from grapes, all or most of the sugar comes from the fruit itself. Brandy is distilled (turned into spirit) from wine. In the brewing of beer and distilling of whisky, sugar is added to the process. Rum, another popular spirit drink, is distilled straight from fermented cane sugar or molasses. The name 'rum' probably comes from an older word 'rumbullion', meaning 'great tumult' – quite a good way of describing the bubbling and boiling that often takes place during fermentation.

We know that drinking too much alcohol will ruin our health, but too many sugary or starchy foods can be bad for us too. Sugar is high in calories and if we consume more calories than we burn up as energy during exercise, our body stores the excess calories as fat – much as beet stores sugar in its large, fat root. In Britain and other Western countries today, many people are overweight because they consume too much sugar, starch or alcohol, and do not take enough exercise. Heart disease and high blood pressure are just two of the ailments over-weight people may suffer from.

Sugar can also be dangerous for people suffering from diabetes, an illness caused by too much sugar in the blood.

Inside a whisky distillery in Scotland.

Most of the sugar used in wine making comes from the grapes. These are vineyards on the banks of the River Rhine in West Germany.

15. The many uses of sugar

Bagasse *(the residue of crushed sugar cane) can be turned into a pulp to make paper for newsprint.*

Sugar and its by-products have an amazing range of uses outside the realm of food and drink.

We have already noted that *bagasse* – the fibrous residue of crushed cane sugar – is used as a fuel in some sugar factories. It can also be turned into a pulp, to form the basis of paper, especially that used for newspapers. It can also be pulped, mixed with resin and made into hardboard. Mixed with molasses it becomes animal feed or fertilizer.

Sugar itself helps in the curing or preserving of leather and tobacco. In the chemical industry, it is converted into substances used in the manufacture of paints, resins and such plastics

Sugar is also used in the curing of leather.

Alcohol, made from sugar, is used instead of petrol to power some cars in Brazil.

as nylon, rayon and polyvinyl chloride (PVC). PVC is used widely in both the electrical and clothing industries. In Brazil, which grows large quantities of sugar cane, sugar converted into alcohol is used as a petrol substitute.

In medicine, too, sugar plays an important role. Cultures of penicillin and other antibiotic drugs are grown on sugar solutions. A liquid product of sugar, called dextran, is sometimes used instead of blood in transfusions. In such cases, there is no problem with matching blood groups, and no risk of transferring any other disease through the blood. Dextran, being a sugar extract, is also a valuable source of energy for sick and weakened patients.

35

16. The history of sugar

The story of sugar goes back to prehistoric times, when men and women gathered fruit and honey (despite the risk of being stung!). For thousands of years, indeed, honey was the only known sweetener, a highly prized commodity, mentioned several times in the Bible. Some people still think that honey is better to eat than refined sugar.

It was somewhere in the Far East that sugar from cane was first produced, about five thousand years ago. The production of cane sugar gradually spread, notably to India, where it was called *sarkara*. Through the centuries, this word changed to the Arabic *sukkar*, then the Latin *saccharum*, and finally to our own word 'sugar'. We also have 'saccharin', a sugar substitute used in some foodstuffs.

Alexander the Great learned about sugar when he invaded Persia and north-west India in 326 BC, and it was imported, first by the Greeks and then by the Romans.

The Muslims tasted the delights of sugar when they conquered Persia in the seventh century AD. Its cultivation then spread across North Africa and into Spain. The Arabs also invented a jelly-like sugar syrup, called *kurat al milh*, from which comes our word 'caramel'.

Left *Before the discovery of sugar, honey was the only known sweetener. This is a picture from an Anglo-Saxon manuscript and shows bees returning to their hives.*

Right *Alexander the Great learned about sugar when he invaded Persia and north-west India in the third century AD. The Greeks were the first people to start importing sugar into continental Europe. Sugar probably first arrived at ports like this one.*

17. The spread of 'white gold'

Several other big events in history helped to spread the cultivation and production of cane sugar around the world. In the Middle Ages, crusaders who had fought in the Holy Land (Palestine in the Middle East) brought samples of sugar back to Europe. As a result there grew up a trade in sugar between Europe and the Middle East, though it remained a rare luxury, which was enjoyed only by kings and queens and the very rich.

Then in 1493, Christopher Columbus planted some sugar cane on the Caribbean island of Santo Domingo. The climate proved ideal for its growth, and soon the whole Caribbean region became the world's largest producer of cane sugar.

There was an unhappy side to the story. African slaves, shipped across the Atlantic, toiled in the hot plantations, while the owners grew rich on the 'white gold', as the refined sugar was called. British, Spanish, French and Dutch colonists went to war over the rich trade in sugar.

At the same time they created new plantations right across the tropics, from Africa to the Far East, so bringing the sugar industry back to the place where it had all started.

From about 1700 onwards, more and more people could afford to buy sugar, despite the fact that for many years the governments of Britain and other European countries taxed it as a luxury, along with rum and tobacco.

In the Middle Ages, crusaders like these, fought in the Holy Land and brought back samples of sugar to Europe.

18. Napoleon intervenes

Sugar beet was grown in ancient times, though only as a vegetable. People took a long time to recognize its sugary properties.

Back in 1575 the French agriculturalist Olivier de Serres wrote of the plant: 'The juice it gives out in cooking is like a sugar syrup'. But it was another two hundred years before scientists found an efficient way of extracting the sugar from beet.

The big breakthrough for sugar beet came in the early nineteenth century, at the time of the Napoleonic Wars. Britain declared war on France, and British warships blockaded many French and other continental ports, so cutting off the supply of cane sugar from the Caribbean

Napoleon (on the white horse) laid the foundations of the sugar industry in Europe today.

and elsewhere. Napoleon responded by ordering the production of sugar from home-grown sugar beet.

His action revolutionized the sugar industry. By the end of the nineteenth century, beet was providing France and other European countries with a large part of their sugar. It was also being widely cultivated in other parts of the world, notably in the USA and Canada.

Britain continued to import cheap cane sugar from parts of its empire up to the time of the First World War (1914–18). As a result of big shipping losses during the war, the British government then followed Napoleon's example and encouraged farmers at home to grow more sugar beet. Today, Britain is also a major sugar beet producer.

During the Napoleonic Wars, British warships blockaded many continental ports.

Above *A gigantic line of harvested French beet awaiting transportation to the factory.*

19. The sugar industry today

Sugar today is a multi-million-pound world industry. This is a plantation on the island of Trinidad, in the Caribbean.

Today growing and producing sugar is a multi-million pound world industry. In the developing countries especially – in Central America and the Caribbean, Africa, Pakistan and India – it provides work for many thousands of people, and boosts their economies in a big way.

Sugar companies have built many schools and hospitals, first and foremost for their employees, but which are often open to the whole local community. They have also built dams or reservoirs to ensure water supplies to factories, roads and railways to carry their products to harbours or docks for export. Such schemes have all brought new jobs and wealth to the countries concerned.

Governments have long recognized the world-wide importance of the sugar industry, and have sought to control it by international agreements. The Brussels Convention of 1903 first set limits to the production of both cane sugar and sugar beet, so as to avoid over-production, a fall in prices and loss of jobs. Further International Sugar Agreements and British Commonwealth Sugar Agreements have followed since then.

British entry into the European Economic Community (EEC) in 1973 brought with it another important agreement on sugar. This was aimed at protecting both the cane sugar producers of many Commonwealth countries, and also sugar beet production within the Community.

In the USA, a Sugar Act of 1948 similarly regulates the production of sugar, by assessing market requirements and regulating the amount farmers and refineries can produce.

The sugar industry provides jobs for thousands of people around the world. Here are some plantation workers in Brazil.

Facts and figures

Sugar production

This chart shows the main sugar-growing countries of the world and the amounts of sugar they produce each year.

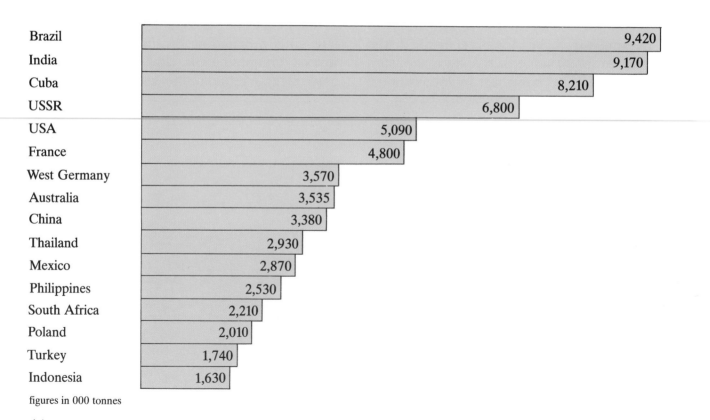

Country	Production
Brazil	9,420
India	9,170
Cuba	8,210
USSR	6,800
USA	5,090
France	4,800
West Germany	3,570
Australia	3,535
China	3,380
Thailand	2,930
Mexico	2,870
Philippines	2,530
South Africa	2,210
Poland	2,010
Turkey	1,740
Indonesia	1,630

figures in 000 tonnes

Important dates

4th century BC   Alexander the Great reached India and brought news of sugar cane to Europe.

926   The first cargo of sugar unloaded in Venice.

1099   The Crusaders discovered sugar cane in Syria and the sugar that came from it. The sugar was brought back to Britain and sold in apothecaries (chemists) at very high prices: about £20 per pound at modern-day prices.

1400s   Spain and Portugal began to grow sugar cane after canes were imported from Sicily. The Portuguese later took sugar cane to Madeira, the Cape Verde Islands, and then to Brazil.

1493   Christopher Columbus took some sugar cane to the Caribbean island of Santo Domingo. Soon it was growing in Cuba, Mexico and the West Indies. Meanwhile, Dutch and French colonists took sugar cane to the islands of the Indian Ocean and of Indonesia. Sugar cane also reached the Philippines, the South Pacific islands and Australasia.

1747   A German chemist succeeded in extracting sugar from beet.

1750   By this date there were 120 sugar refineries in Britain, which produced about 30,000 tonnes of sugar a year. Sugar beet was still unknown as a source of sugar.

1786   Several small sugar beet refineries were started in Silesia, in central Europe.

1811   Unable to obtain sugar from the French colonies because of a blockade by the British fleet, Napoleon ordered large areas of France to be sown with beet.

1815   Some £3 million was raised by the British government from its tax on sugar, which was still considered a luxury.

1832   The first sugar beet refinery was opened in Britain, but it was not a commercial success.

1874   Gladstone withdrew the British tax on sugar. This meant that the poorer classes could afford to buy it for the first time.

1880   By this date, sugar beet had displaced cane as the main source of sugar in Europe, and the growing of beet had spread to every temperate zone, including the USA and Canada.

1925   This year saw the start of the sugar beet industry in Britain.

45

Glossary

Affination Part of the sugar-refining process, separating molasses from sugar crystals. The word means 'closely connected'.

Antibiotics Substances, such as penicillin, that attack living organisms, including very harmful bacteria.

Bagasse French word for the residue of sugar cane after the sugar has been extracted.

Calorie Scientific measure of heat (Latin *calor*) and of heat-energy in food.

Carbohydrates Word meaning carbon and water. Carbohydrates are foodstuffs consisting mainly of starches and sugars. Other types of food are proteins, fats and vitamins.

Caster sugar Finely grained sugar. Named after a type of jar or bottle with small holes in the top, for sprinkling out the contents.

Centrifugal Machine, like a giant spin-drier, that separates sugar crystals from syrup and molasses. Centrifugal force makes objects fly outwards.

Chlorophyll Word from Greek, meaning 'green leaf'. Chlorophyll is the green substance in plants that allows photosynthesis to take place.

Commonwealth Community of self-governing countries, once a part of the British Empire.

Crop rotation Changing the crops in fields, so that the soil is not exhausted by the same crop each year.

Diffusion In sugar-making, the extraction of sugar particles from cane or beet by dissolving them in water.

EEC European Economic Community (the Common Market), a trade and political organization, founded in 1957. Britain joined the Community in 1973.

Enzyme A catalyst or agent that triggers off chemical changes. Enzymes are needed in fermentation and photosynthesis.

Fermentation Chemical process by which substances are changed into something else. The best-known type of fermentation changes sugar into alcohol.

Germination Sprouting or budding of a new plant from its seed.

Granulated Made up of small grains, granules or crystals. The standard grade of sugar.

Irrigation Land supplied with water by means of dams, reservoirs, canals, channels and pipes.

Machete Spanish name for the long knife used to cut sugar cane.

Massecuite The mixture of syrup and sugar crystals formed during sugar-making. French for 'cooked mass'.

Molasses Dark, thick syrup, also called 'blackstrap', produced during sugar-making. It is used to make cattle food and rum.

Pectin Natural substance in fruit juice that makes it congeal or set.

Photosynthesis The chemical process by which plants absorb sunlight and store it as sugars and starches. From the Greek words meaning 'light' and 'putting together' or 'building up'.

Sources of further information

If you would like to find out more about the sugar industry, the following organizations produce pamphlets and charts:

British Sugar Bureau
140 Park Lane
London W1Y 3AA

U.S. Beet Sugar Association
1156 Fifteenth Street NW
Washington DC 20025

Australian Sugar Producers Association
GPO Box 608
333 Adelaide Street
Brisbane 4001

Books to read

BALDWIN, D. and LISTER, C. *Your Body Fuel* (Wayland, 1984)
CATHERALL, E. *Energy for Life* (Wayland, 1982)
IVESON-IVESON, J. *Your Teeth* (Wayland, 1985)
LUCAS, D.A. *A Spoonful of Sugar* (Wayland, 1982)
PITT, V. *Sugar* (Franklin Watts, 1974)
WATSON, T. and J. *What the World Eats* series (Wayland, 1982)

Picture acknowledgements

The author and publishers would like to thank the following for allowing their illustrations to be reproduced in this book: The Bodleian Library 36; British Sugar 16; Camerapix Hutchison Library 13 (both), 15 (bottom/Tony Hardwell), 17 (right/ Michael MacIntyre), 22 (Tony Hardwell), 28 (Mick Rock), 41 (top/Mick Rock); Bruce Coleman Ltd 11 (top/ Michael Viard; bottom/Gerald Cubitt), 12 (Jen & Des Bartlett), 14 (Alain Compost), 15 (top/Fritz Prenzel), 29 (Jennifer Fry); Chris Fairclough *frontispiece*, 23; Tate & Lyle 24, 25 (both), 26, 27; TOPHAM 17 (left). The illustrations on pages 8, 10 and 44 were drawn by Malcolm S. Walker. The following illustrations are from the Wayland Picture Library *cover*, 6, 7 (both), 9 (both), 18, 19 (both), 20, 21, 30, 31, 32, 33, 34, 35 (both), 37, 38–9, 40, 42, 43.

Index